# INSECTS UP CLOSE

# Cockroaches

by Patrick Perish

BELLWETHER MEDIA • MINNEAPOLIS, MN

BLASTOFF! READERS

Note to Librarians, Teachers, and Parents:

**Blastoff! Readers** are carefully developed by literacy experts and combine standards-based content with developmentally appropriate text.

**Level 1** provides the most support through repetition of high-frequency words, light text, predictable sentence patterns, and strong visual support.

**Level 2** offers early readers a bit more challenge through varied simple sentences, increased text load, and less repetition of high-frequency words.

**Level 3** advances early-fluent readers toward fluency through increased text and concept load, less reliance on visuals, longer sentences, and more literary language.

**Level 4** builds reading stamina by providing more text per page, increased use of punctuation, greater variation in sentence patterns, and increasingly challenging vocabulary.

**Level 5** encourages children to move from "learning to read" to "reading to learn" by providing even more text, varied writing styles, and less familiar topics.

Whichever book is right for your reader, Blastoff! Readers are the perfect books to build confidence and encourage a love of reading that will last a lifetime!

This edition first published in 2019 by Bellwether Media, Inc.

No part of this publication may be reproduced in whole or in part without written permission of the publisher. For information regarding permission, write to Bellwether Media, Inc., Attention: Permissions Department, 6012 Blue Circle Drive, Minnetonka, MN 55343.

Library of Congress Cataloging-in-Publication Data

Title: Cockroaches / by Patrick Perish.
Description: Minneapolis, MN : Bellwether Media, Inc., [2019] | Series: Blastoff! Readers: Insects Up Close | Includes bibliographical references and index.
Identifiers: LCCN 2017056256 (print) | LCCN 2017058889 (ebook) | ISBN 9781626178021 (hardcover : alk. paper) | ISBN 9781681035277 (ebook)
Subjects: LCSH: Cockroaches–Juvenile literature.
Classification: LCC QL505.5 (ebook) | LCC QL505.5 .P47 2018 (print) | DDC 595.7/28–dc23
LC record available at https://lccn.loc.gov/2017056256

Editor: Christina Leaf      Designer: Tamara JM Peterson

Printed in the United States of America, North Mankato, MN

# Table of Contents

# What Are Cockroaches?

Cockroaches are some of the world's oldest insects. They were around before dinosaurs!

Cockroaches are also called roaches. Most are brown, red, or black. Some have colorful marks.

ACTUAL SIZE:
American cockroach

Cockroaches have flat, oval bodies. They use their long **antennae** to smell.

**antenna**

# Roach Life

Roaches like dark, **damp**, and warm places. Only a few kinds enter homes.

Cockroaches are
not picky eaters.
They eat dead
plants and animals.

# FAVORITE FOOD:

dead leaves

Roaches like to be with other roaches. They gather to eat and sleep.

Most female cockroaches lay their eggs in a case. The eggs **hatch** weeks later.

egg case ⟶

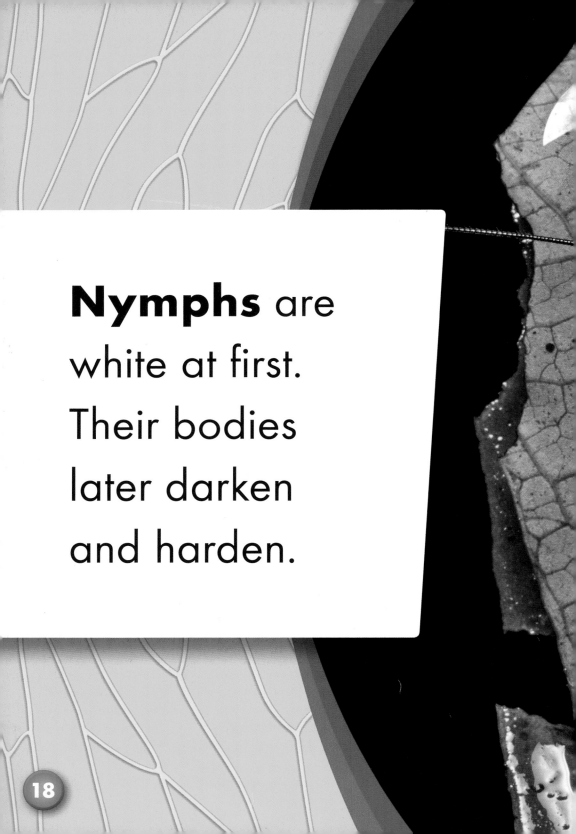

**Nymphs** are white at first. Their bodies later darken and harden.

## COCKROACH LIFE SPAN:

### 1 to 2 years

nymph

Cockroaches **molt** as they grow. Soon they are big, hungry adults!

**molting**

# Glossary

**antennae**

feelers connected to the head that sense information around them

**molt**

to shed skin for growth

**damp**

slightly wet

**nymphs**

young insects; nymphs look like small adults without full wings.

**hatch**

to break out of an egg

# To Learn More

## AT THE LIBRARY

Nelson, Robin. *Crawling Cockroaches*. Minneapolis, Minn.: Lerner Publications, 2017.

Schuetz, Kari. *Hissing Cockroaches*. Minneapolis, Minn.: Bellwether Media, 2016.

Schuh, Mari. *Cockroaches*. Minneapolis, Minn.: Jump!, 2015

## ON THE WEB

Learning more about cockroaches is as easy as 1, 2, 3.

1. Go to www.factsurfer.com.

2. Enter "cockroaches" into the search box.

3. Click the "Surf" button and you will see a list of related web sites.

With factsurfer.com, finding more information is just a click away.

# Index

The images in this book are reproduced through the courtesy of: Aleksey Stemmer, front cover, pp. 6-7; luis2499, pp. 4-5; Damsea, pp. 8-9; SleepyWeaselEntertainment, pp. 10-11; Barnaby Chambers, pp. 12-13; Stocksnapper, p. 13; hayesphotography, pp. 14-15; Kim Taylor/ Alamy, pp. 16-17 (cockroach); stockcreations, pp. 16-17 (background); Guenter Fischer/ Alamy, pp. 18-19, 22 (nymph); NokHoOkNoi, pp. 20-21, 22 (molt); Bates Littlehales/ Getty, p. 22 (hatch); Peter Vandenbelt, p. 22 (damp); ozgur keren bulur, p. 22 (antennae).